My Firs
Valentine's Day

DON'T FORGET TO LEAVE US YOUR

FEEDBACK

Happy Valentine's Day

The Baby Name:

____

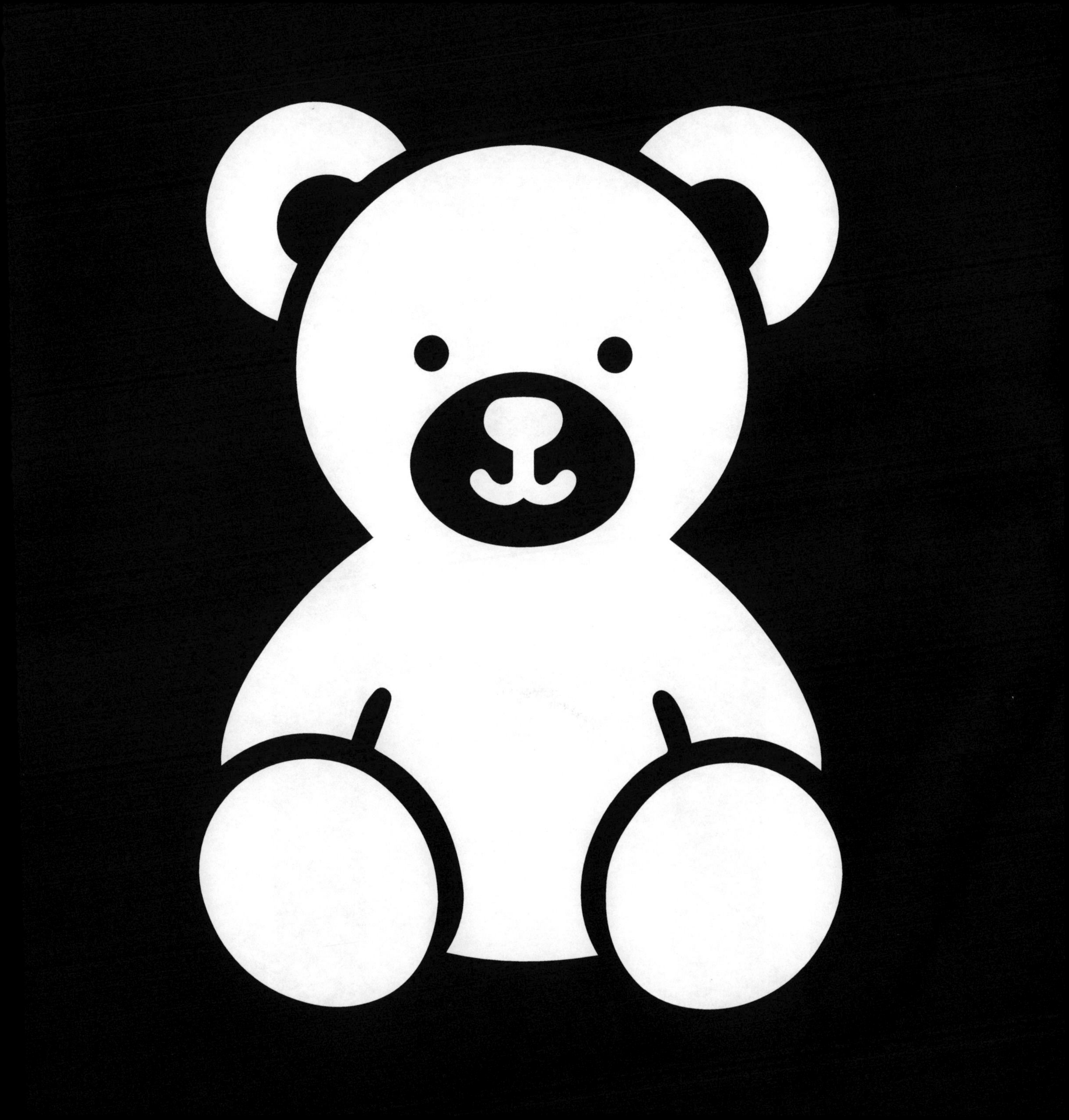

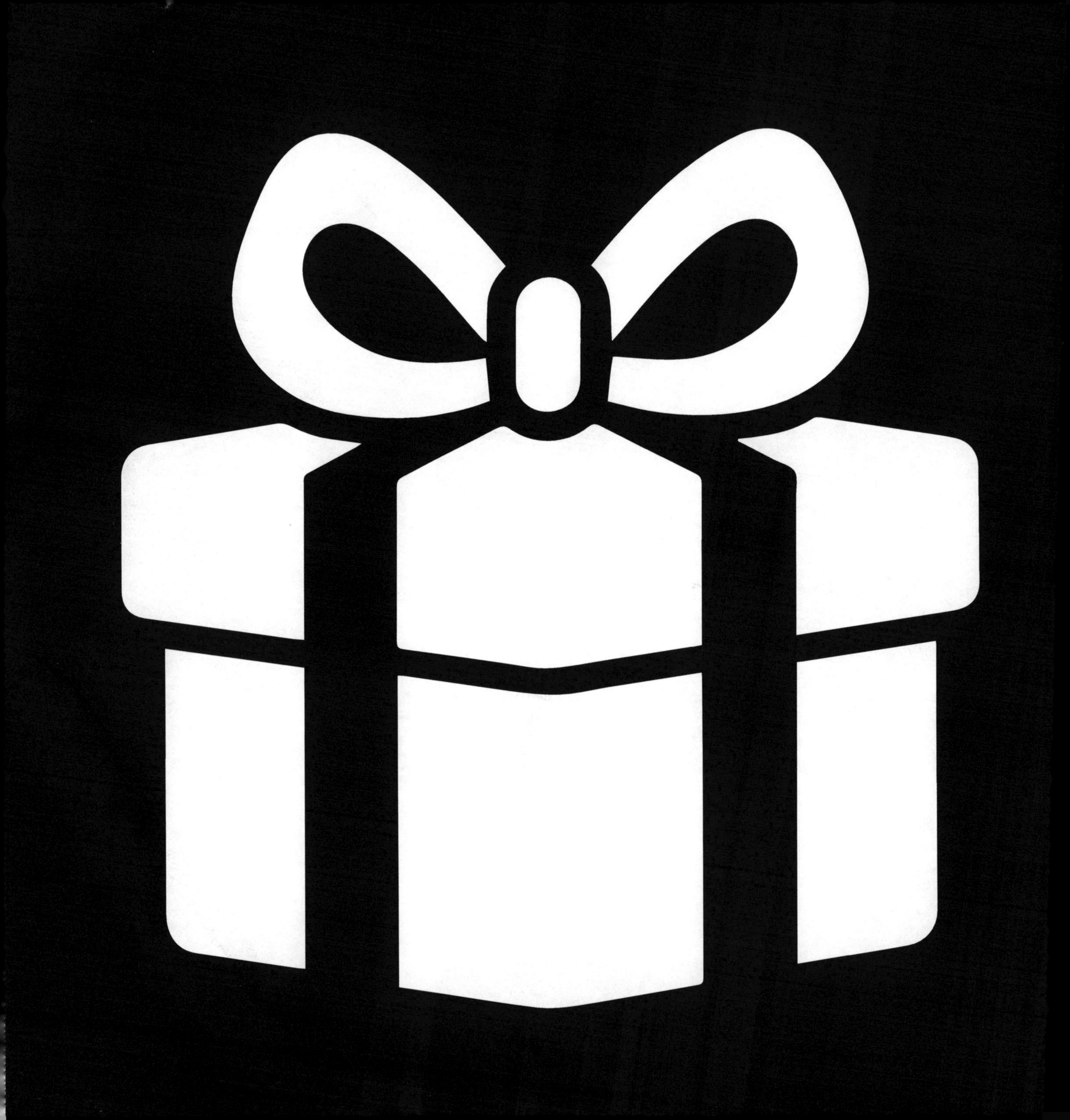

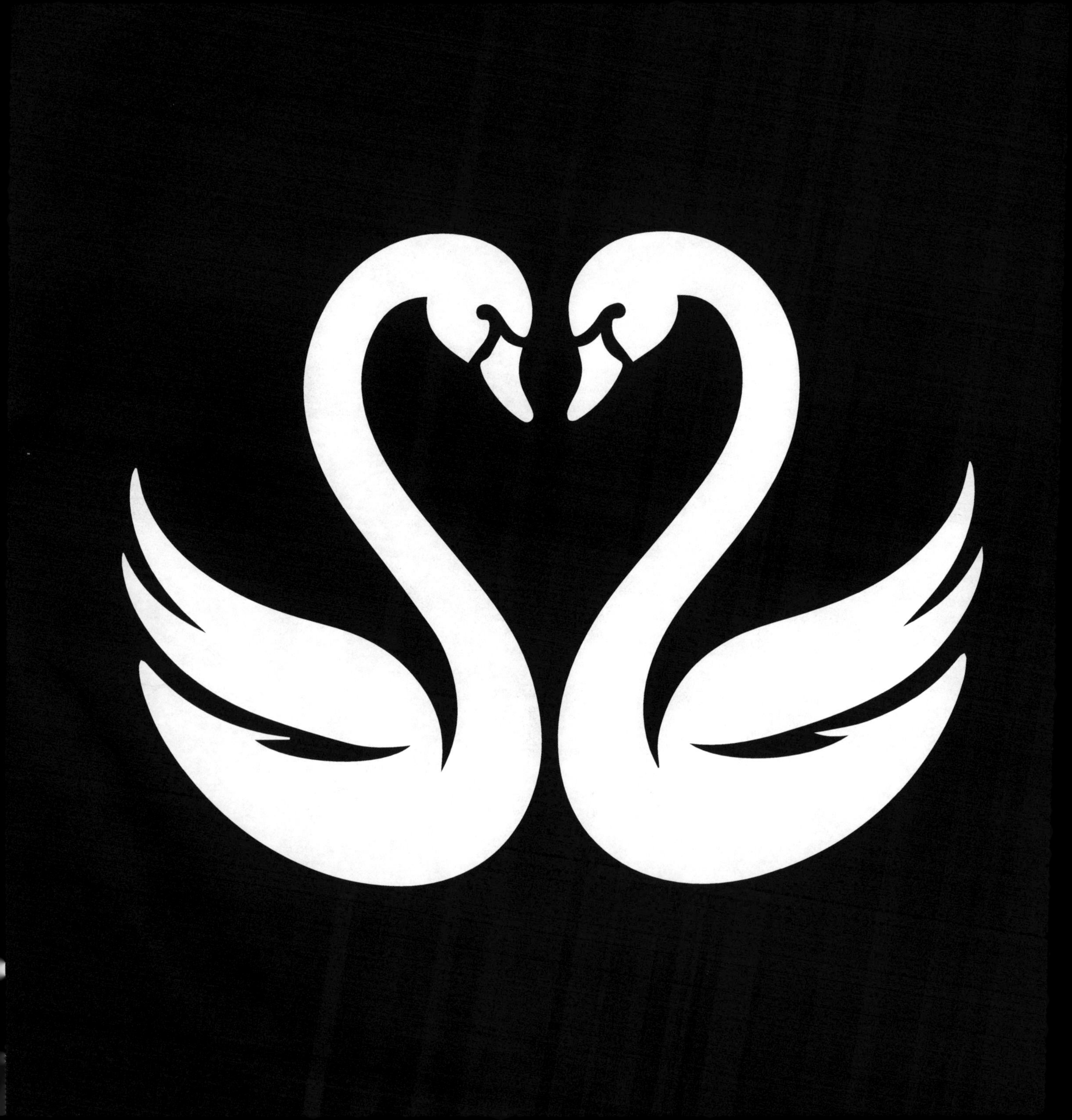

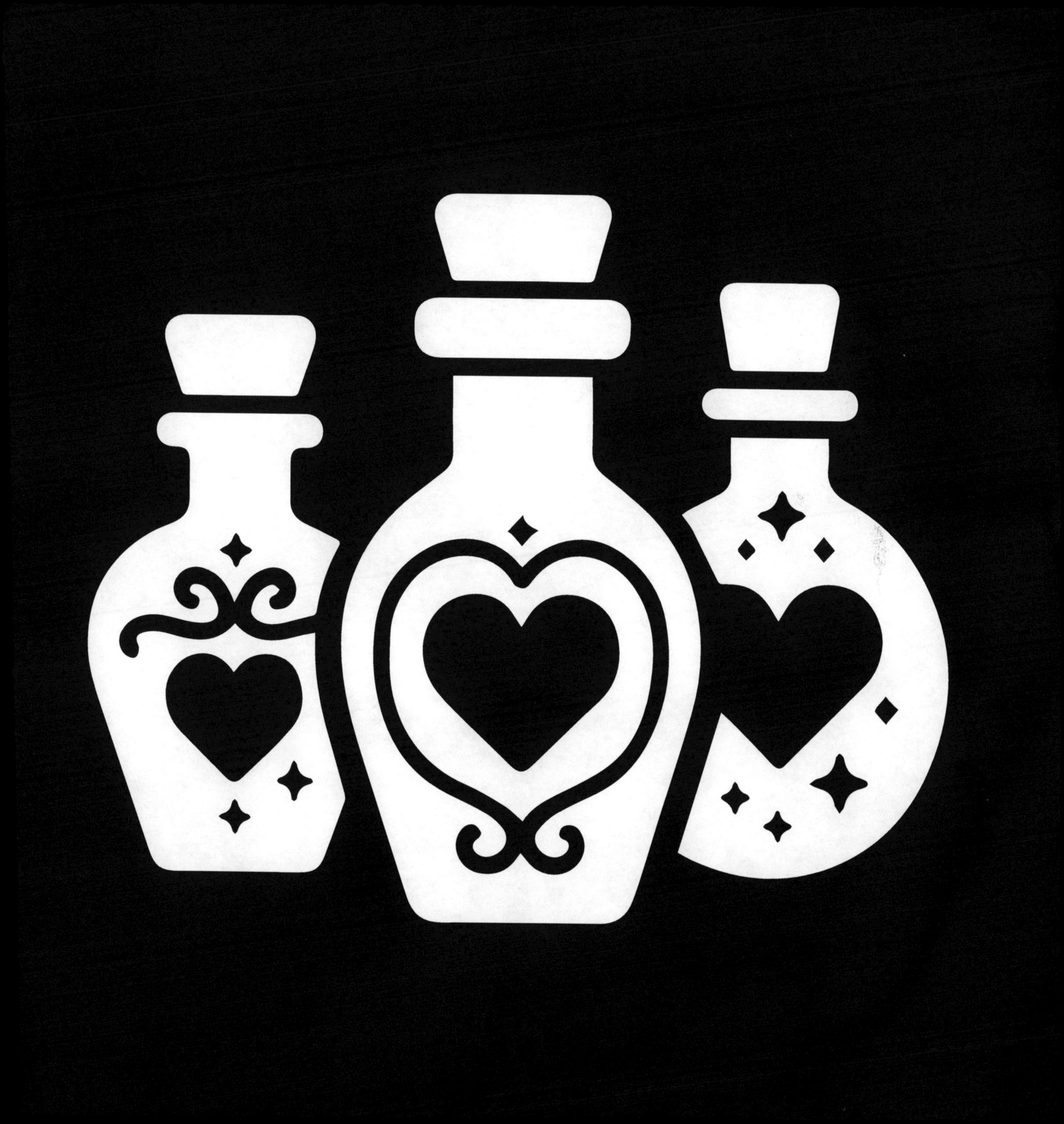

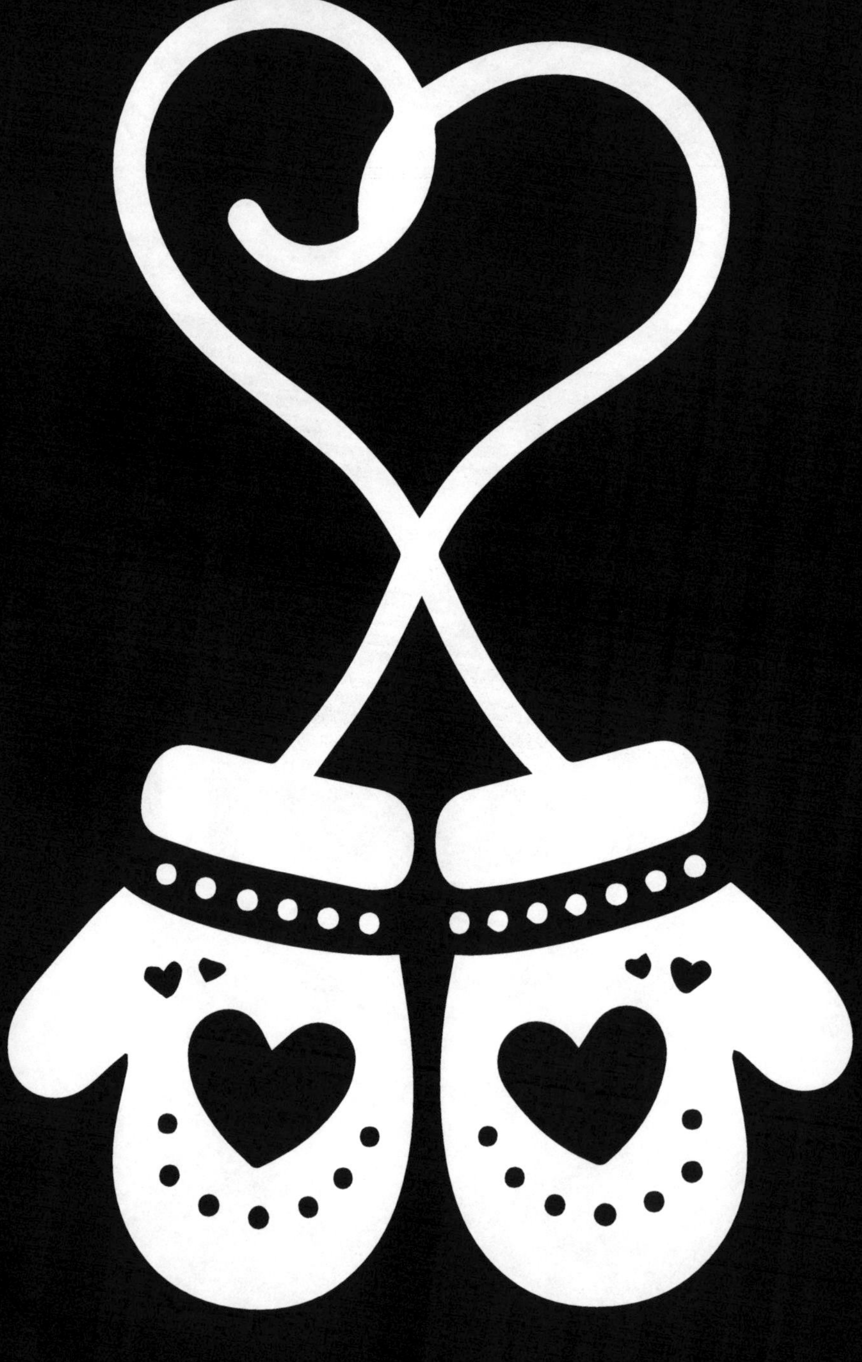

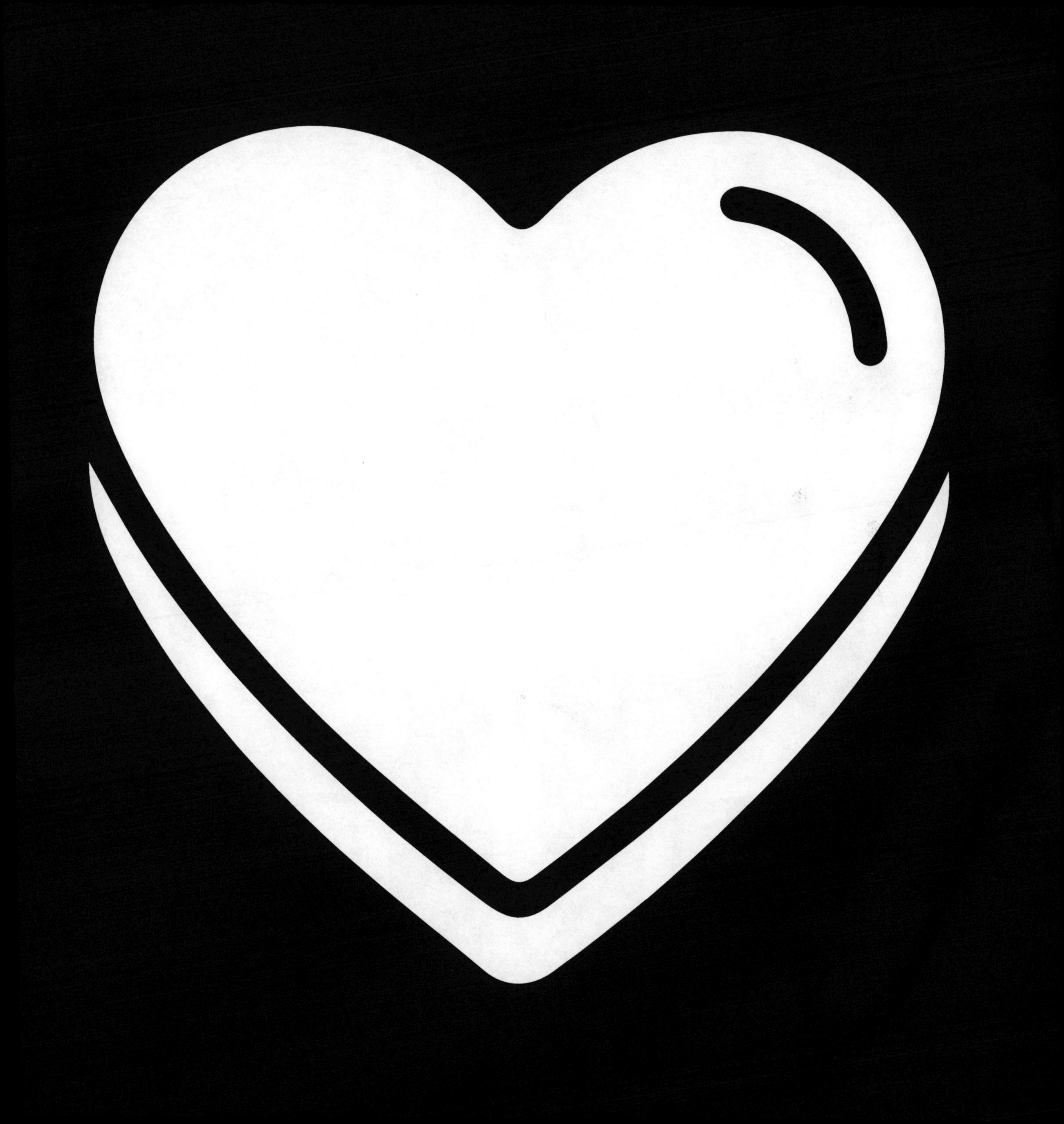

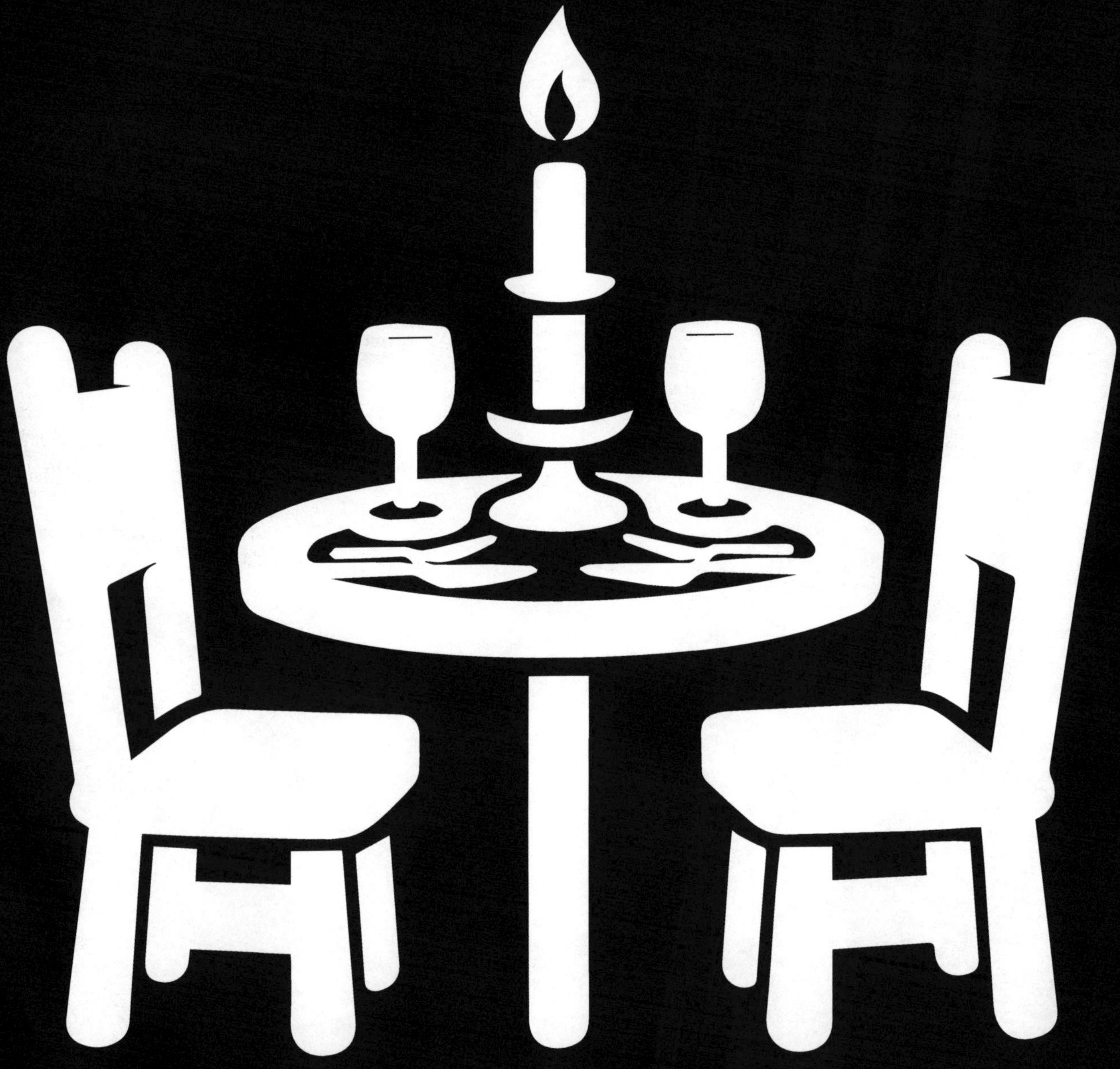

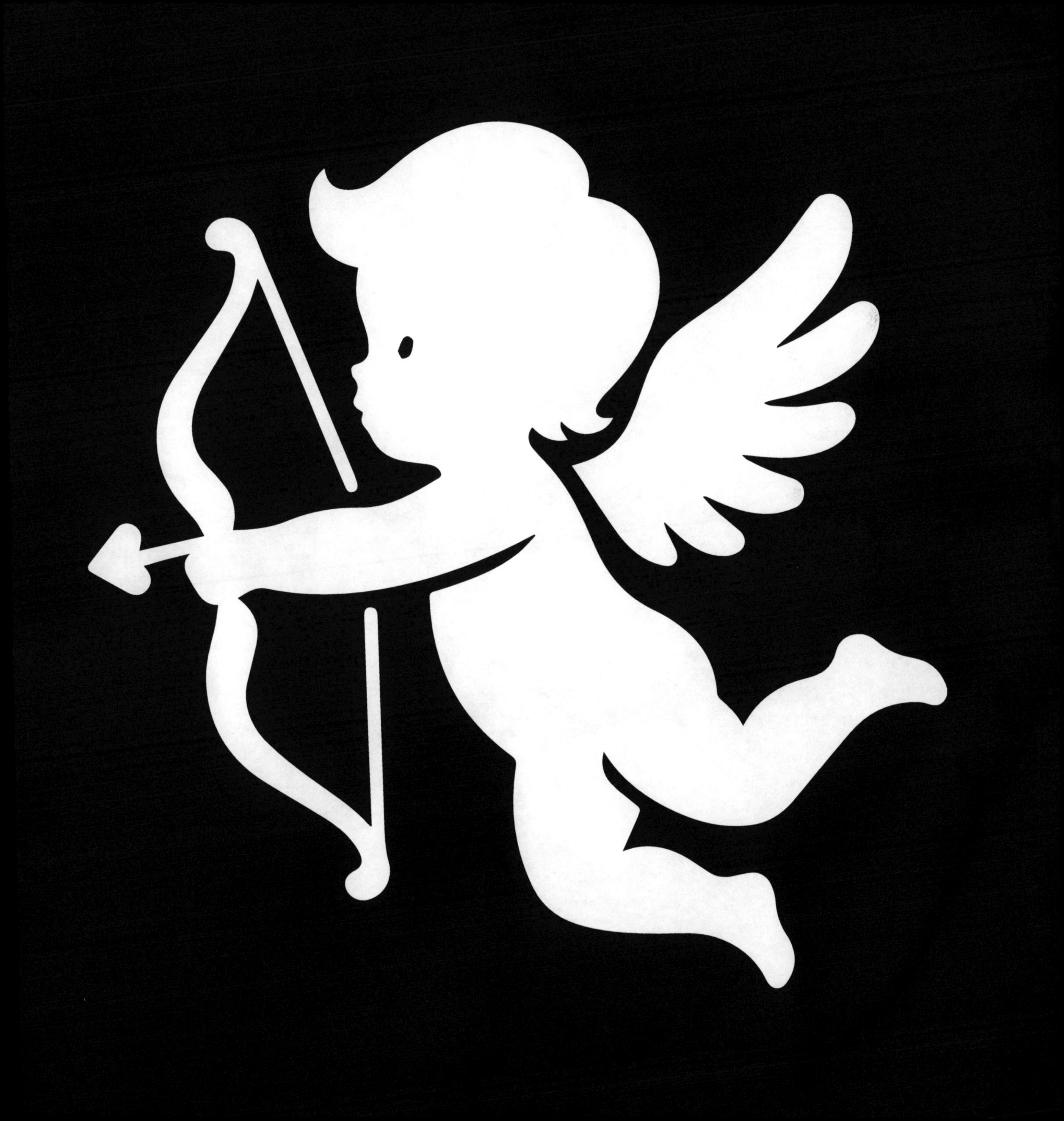

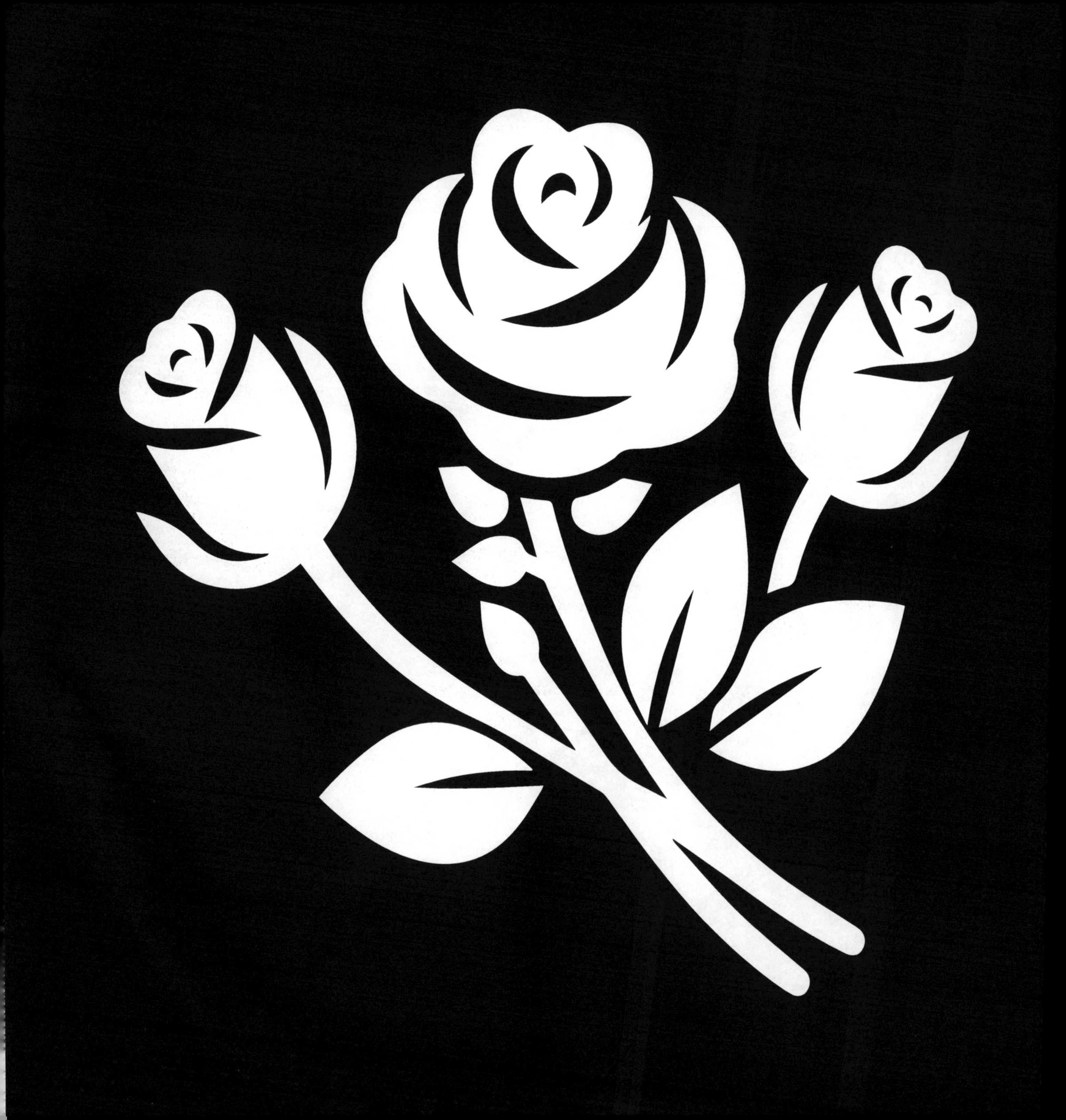

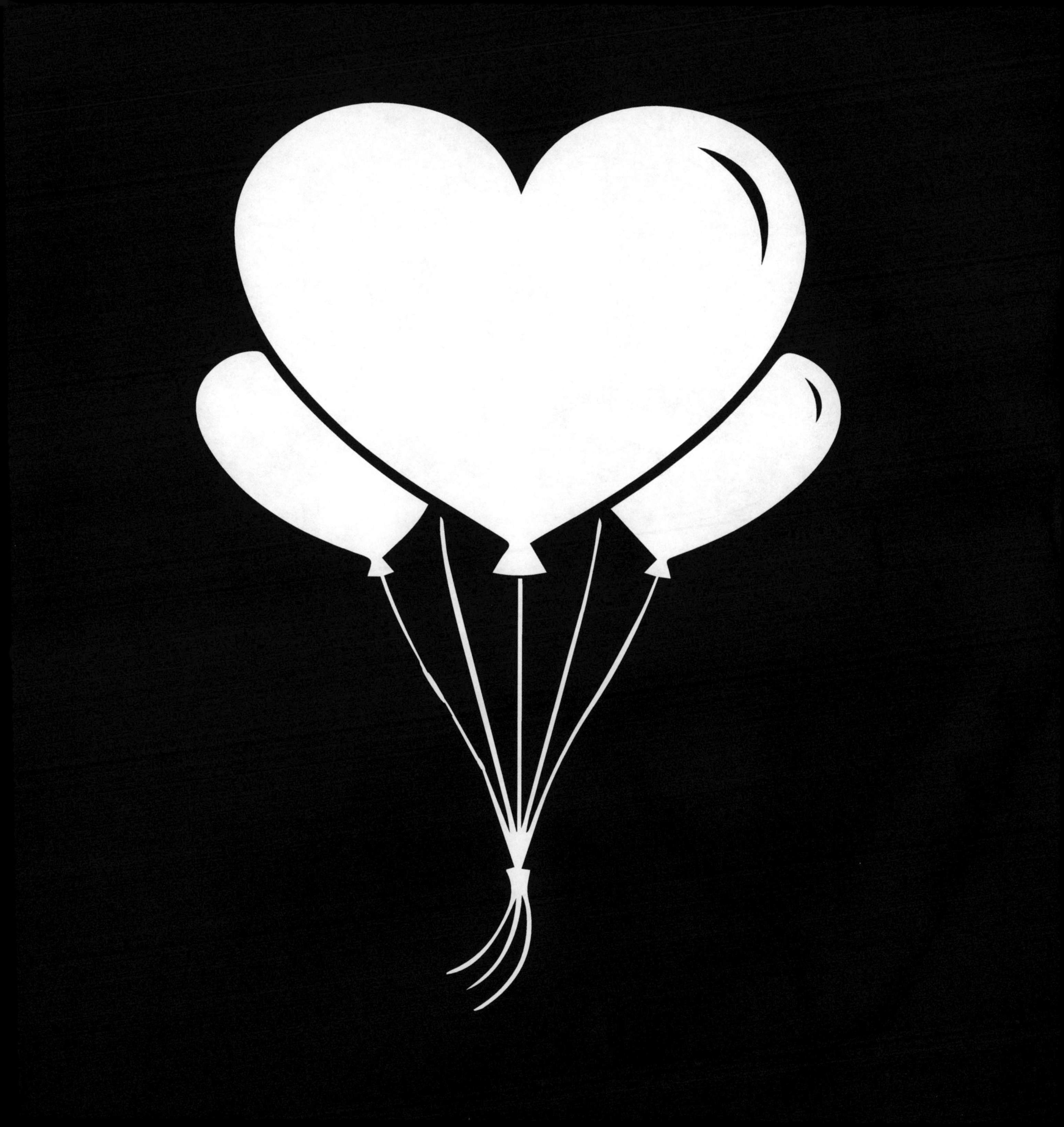

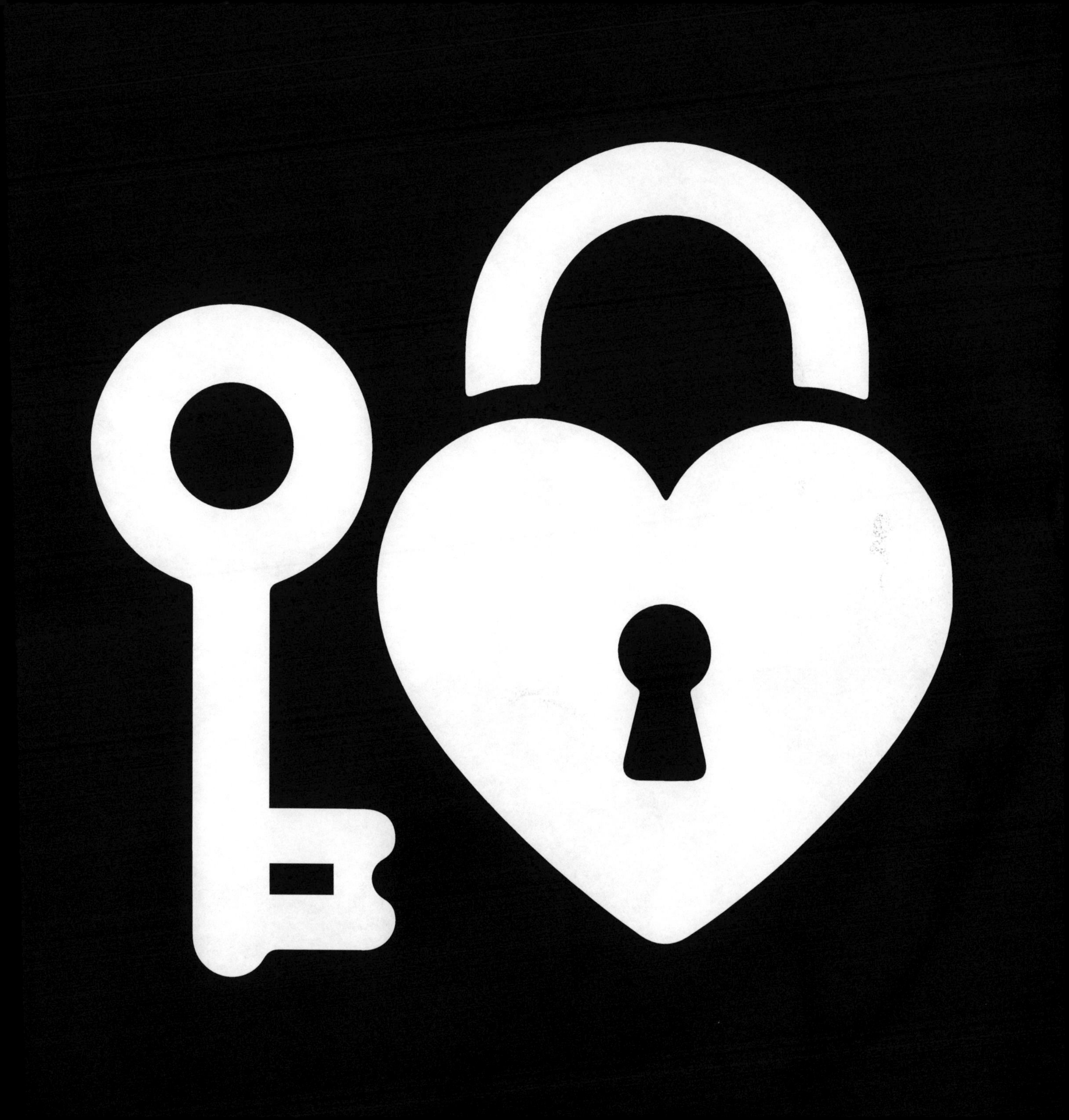

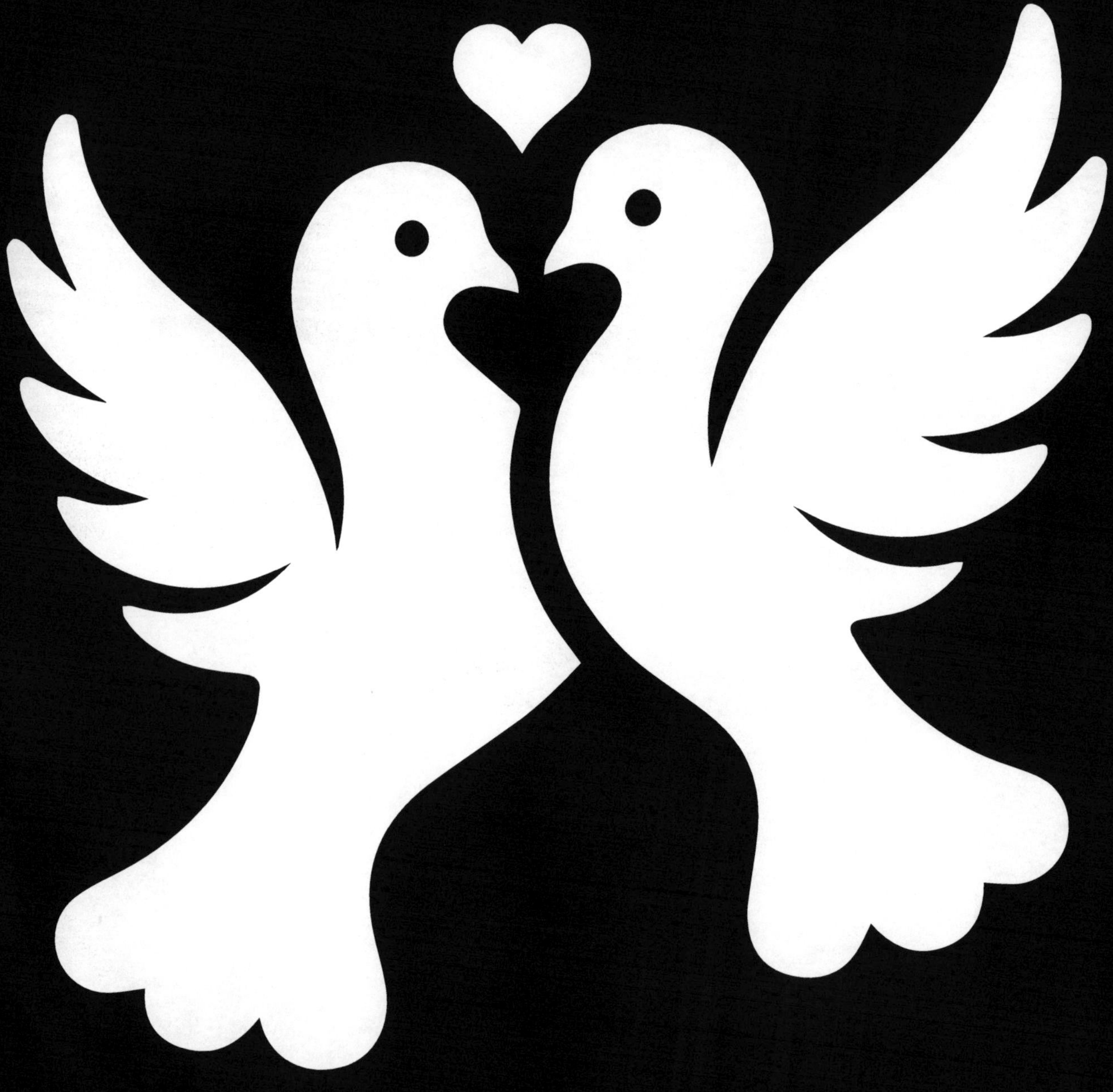

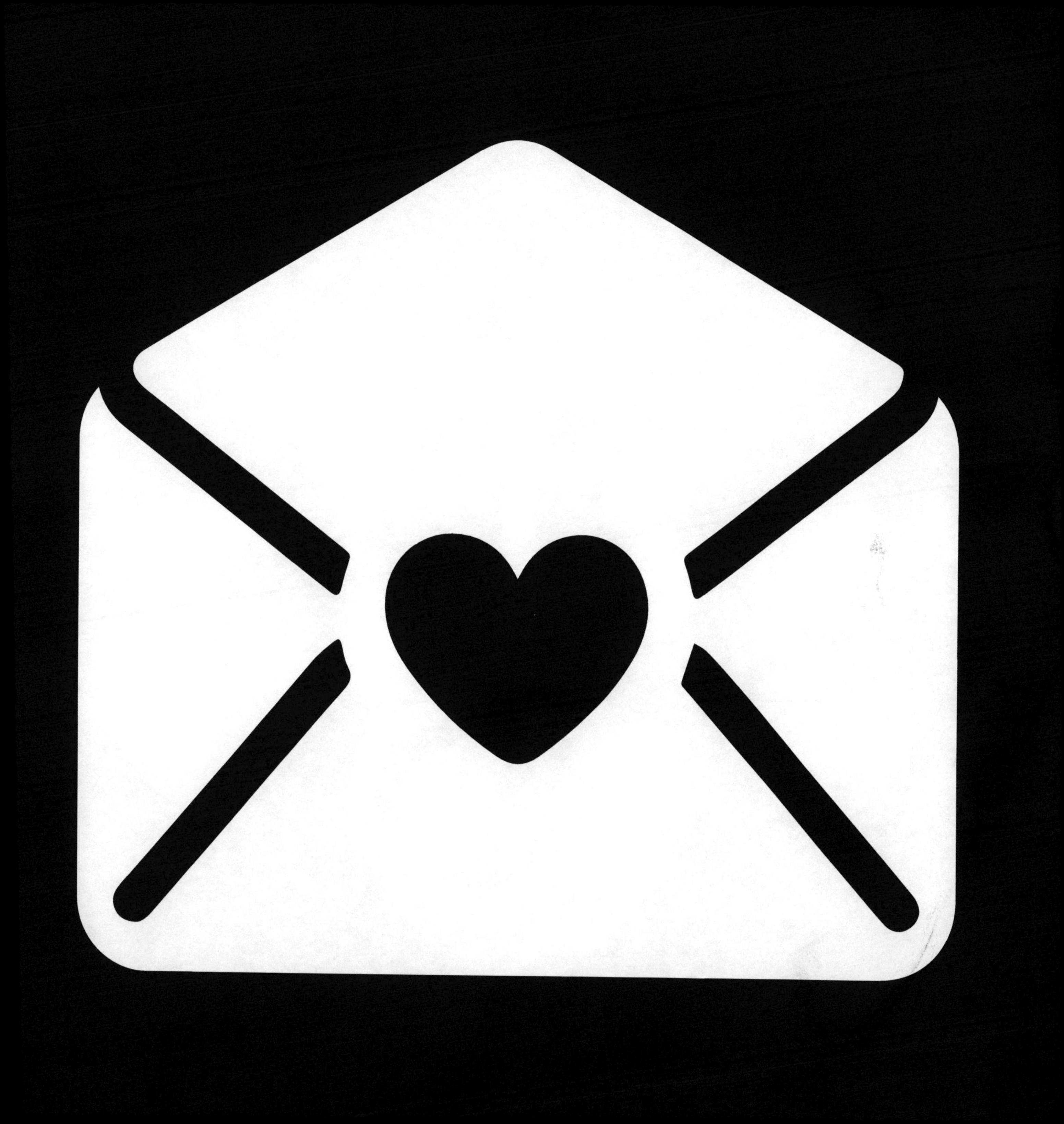

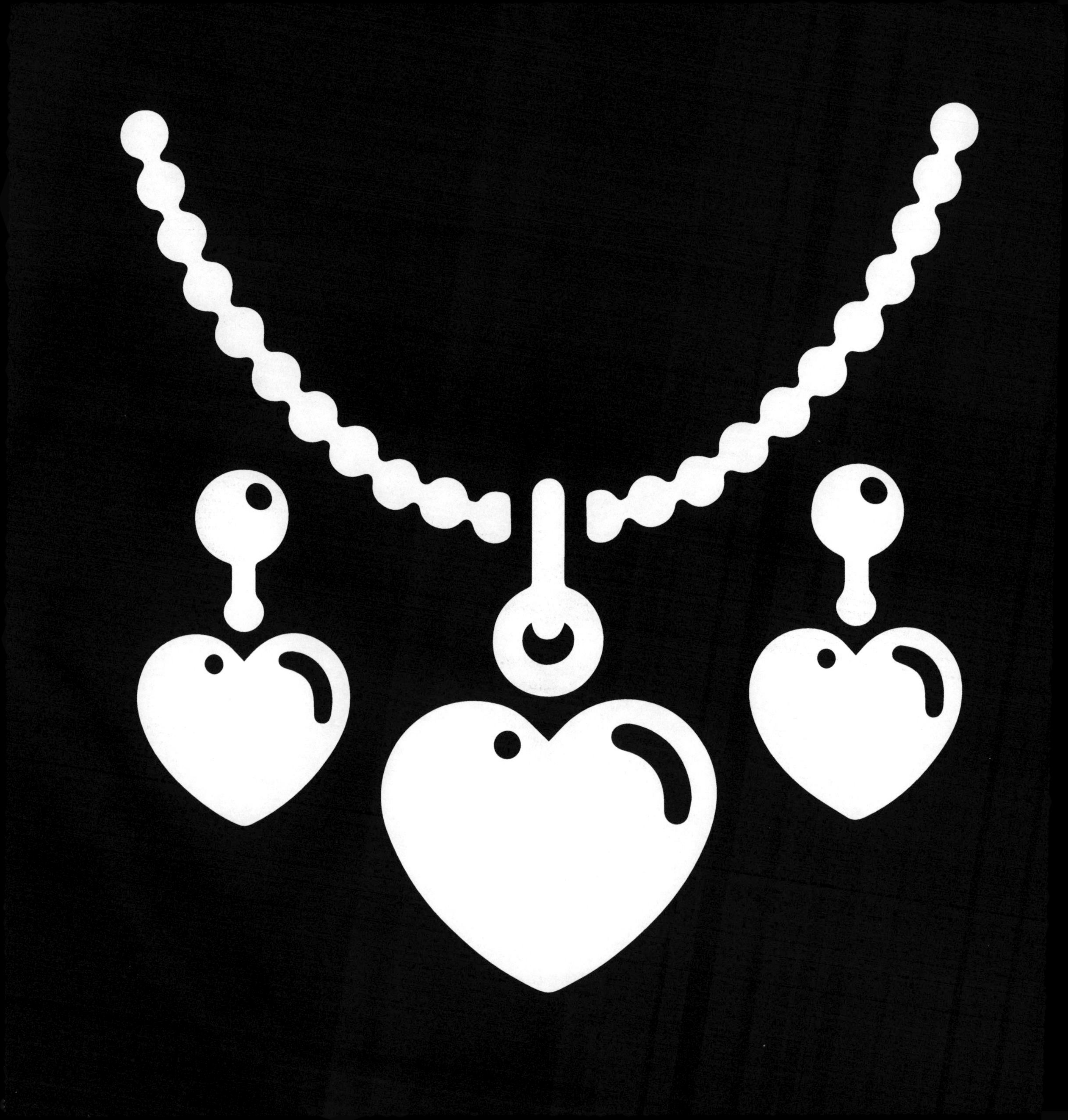

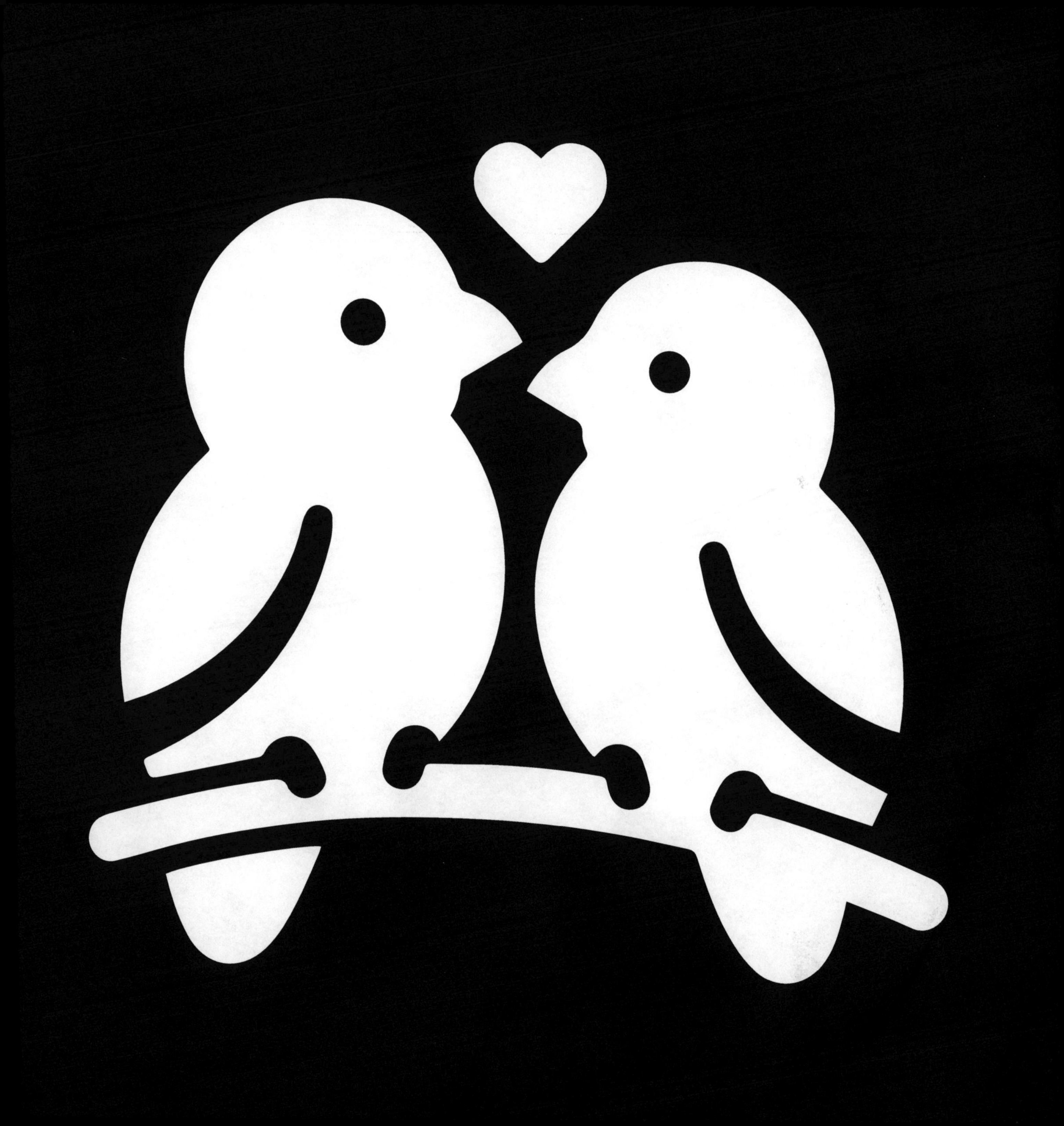

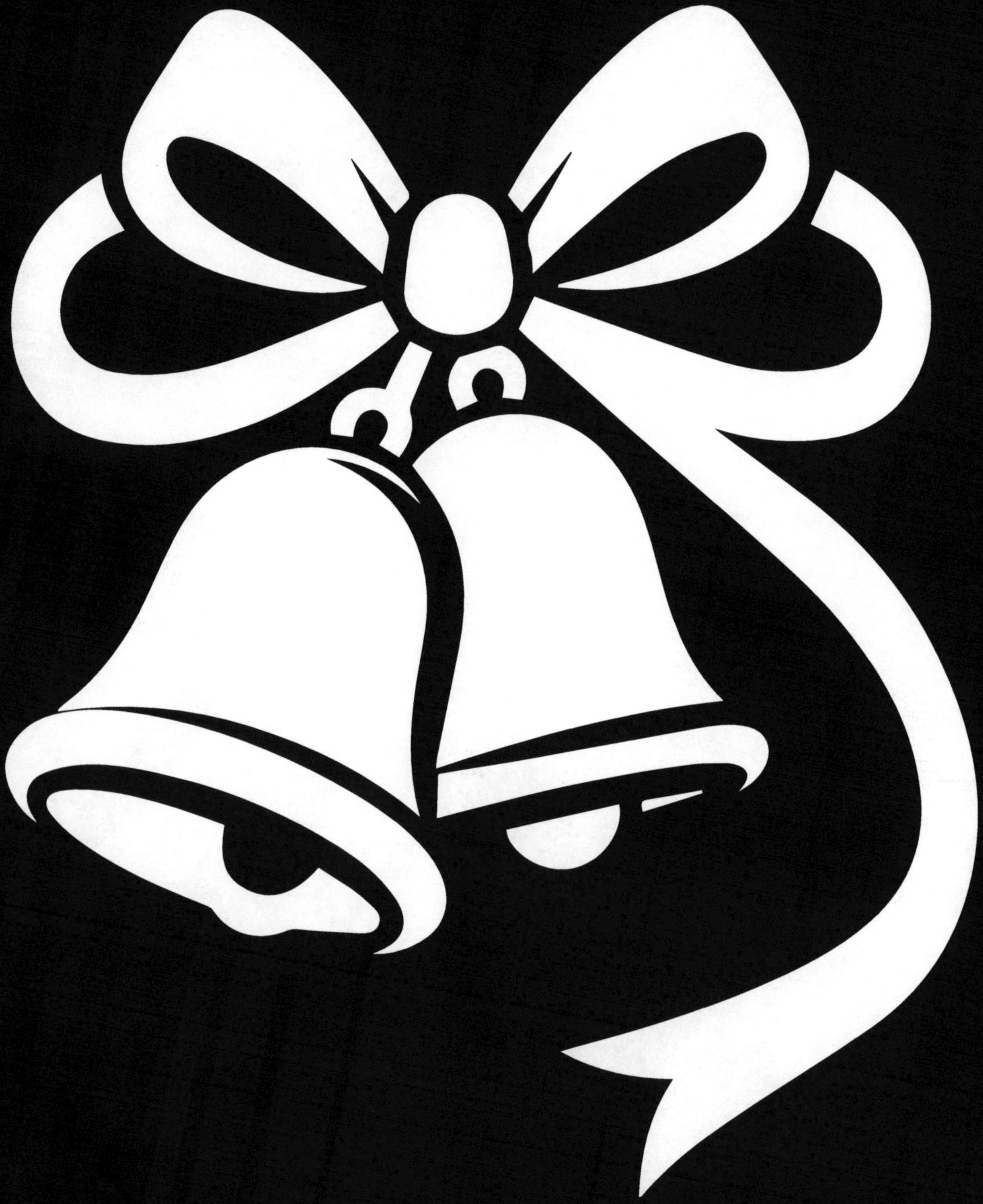

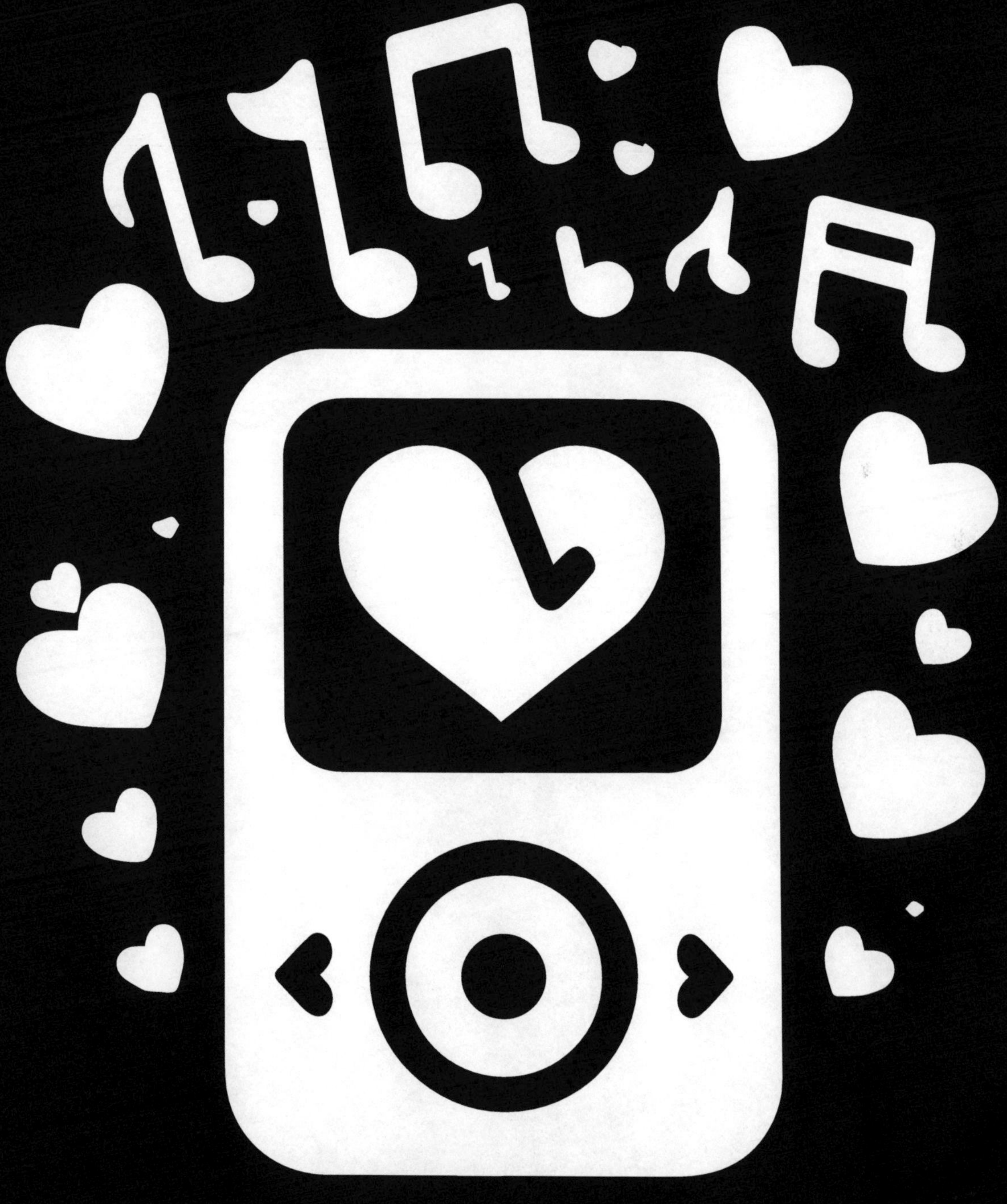

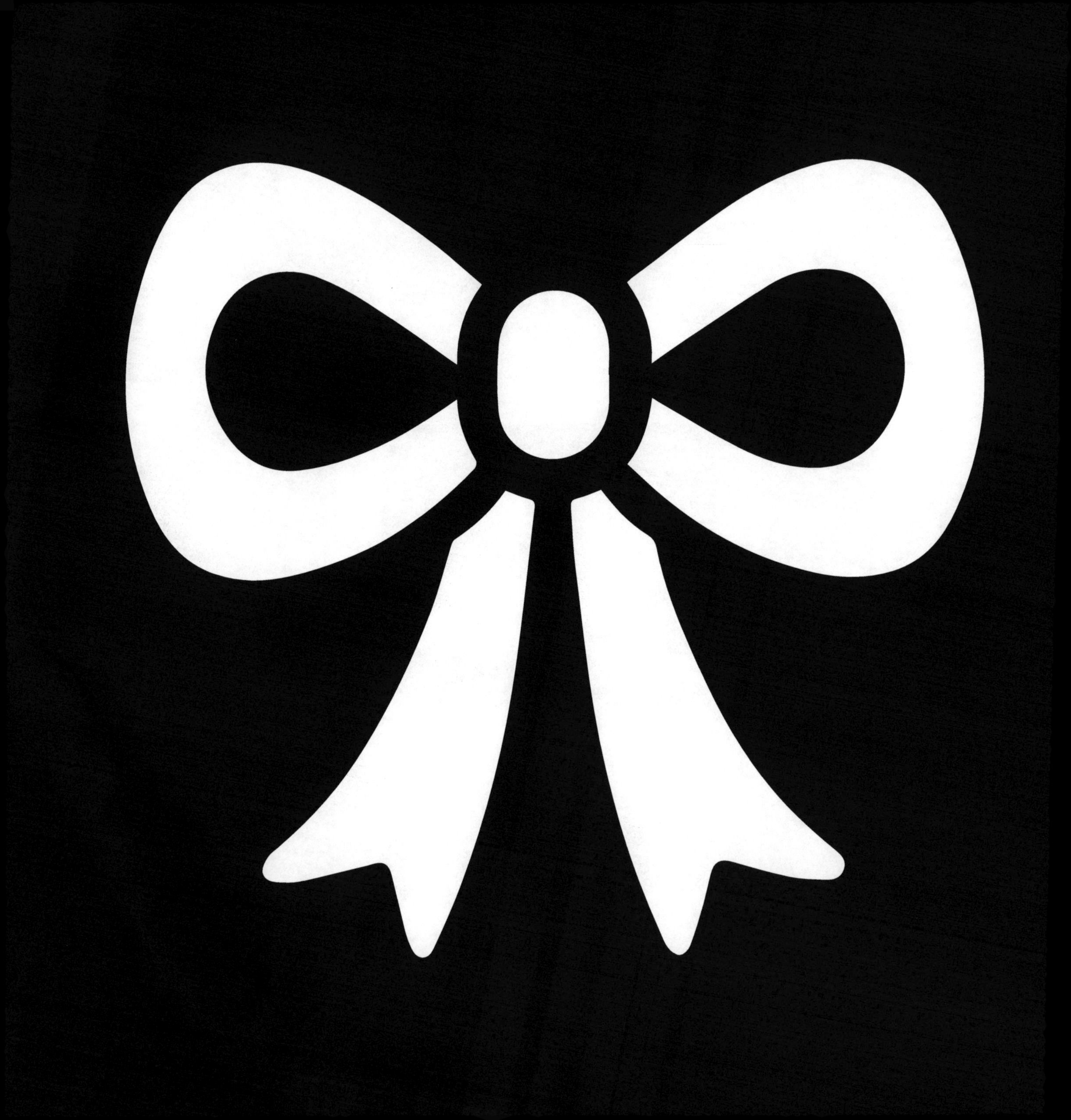

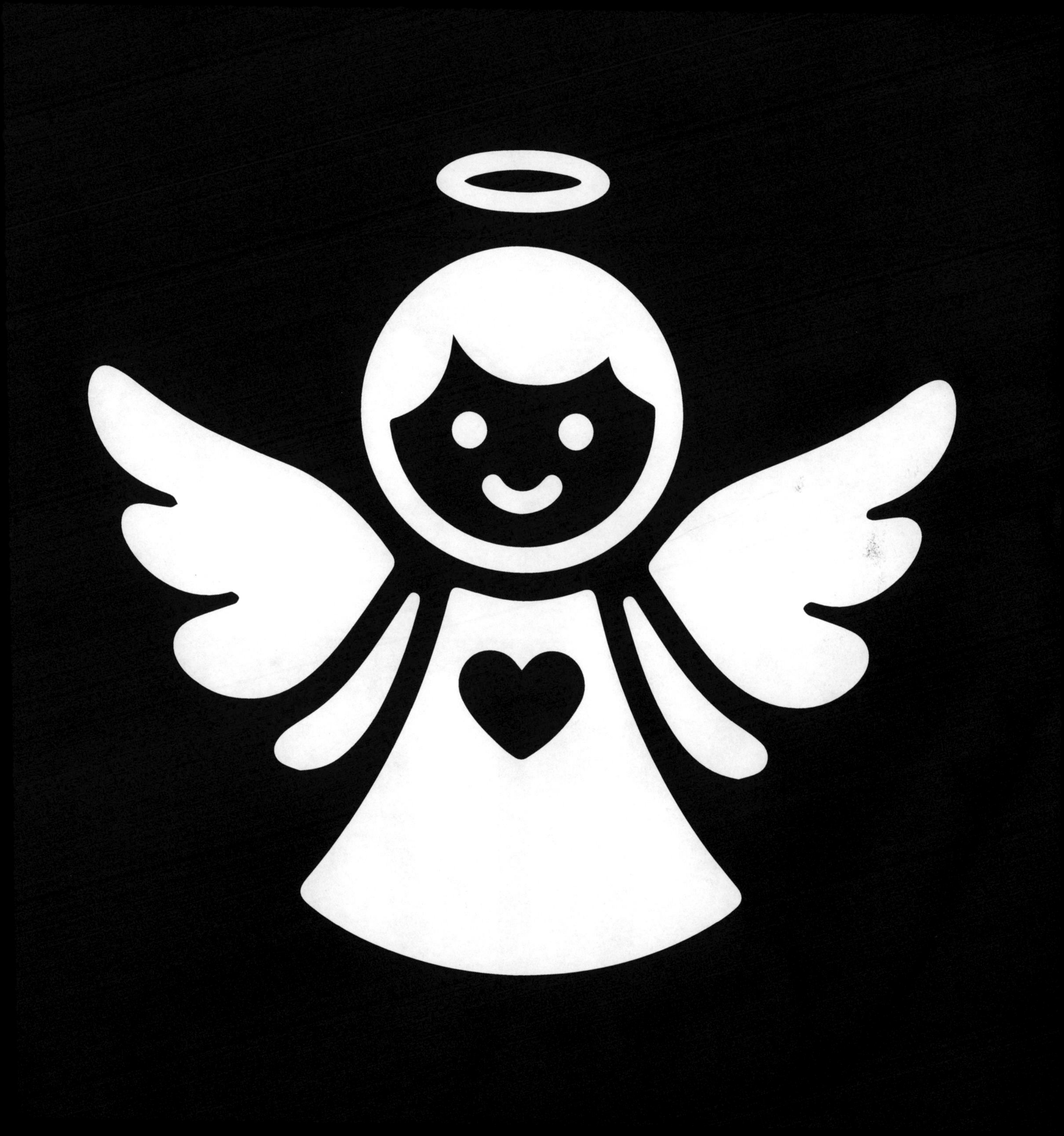

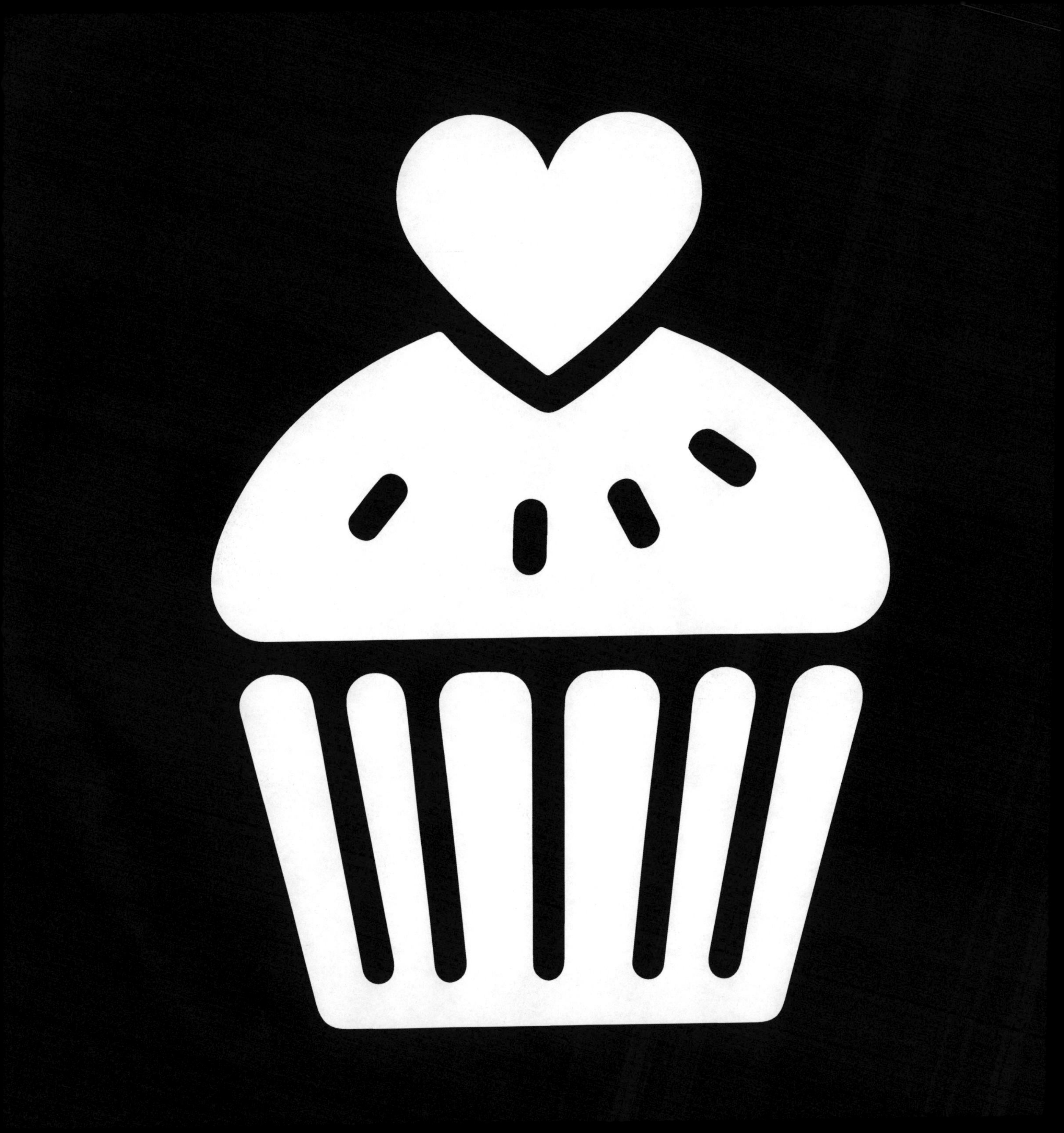

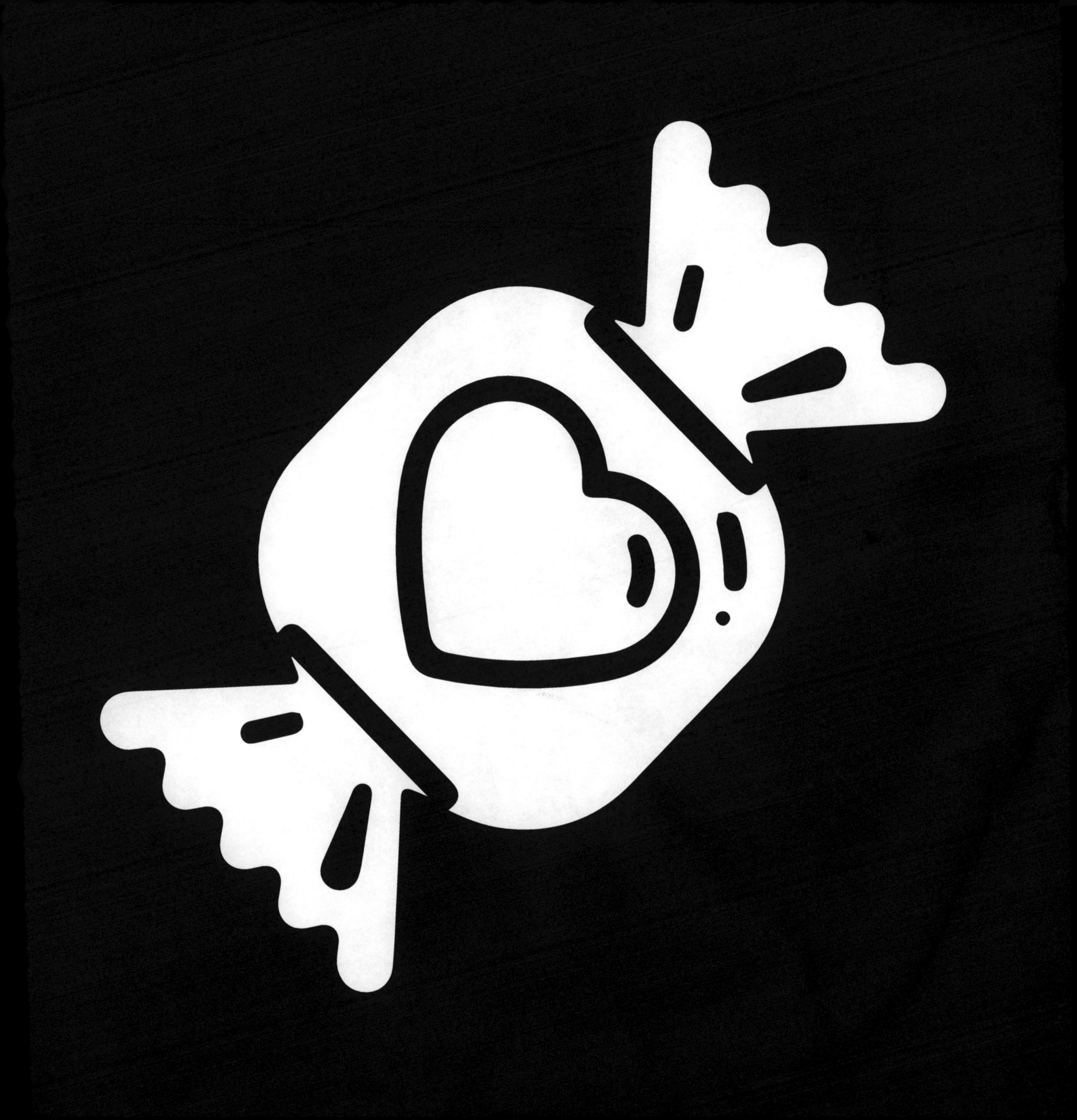

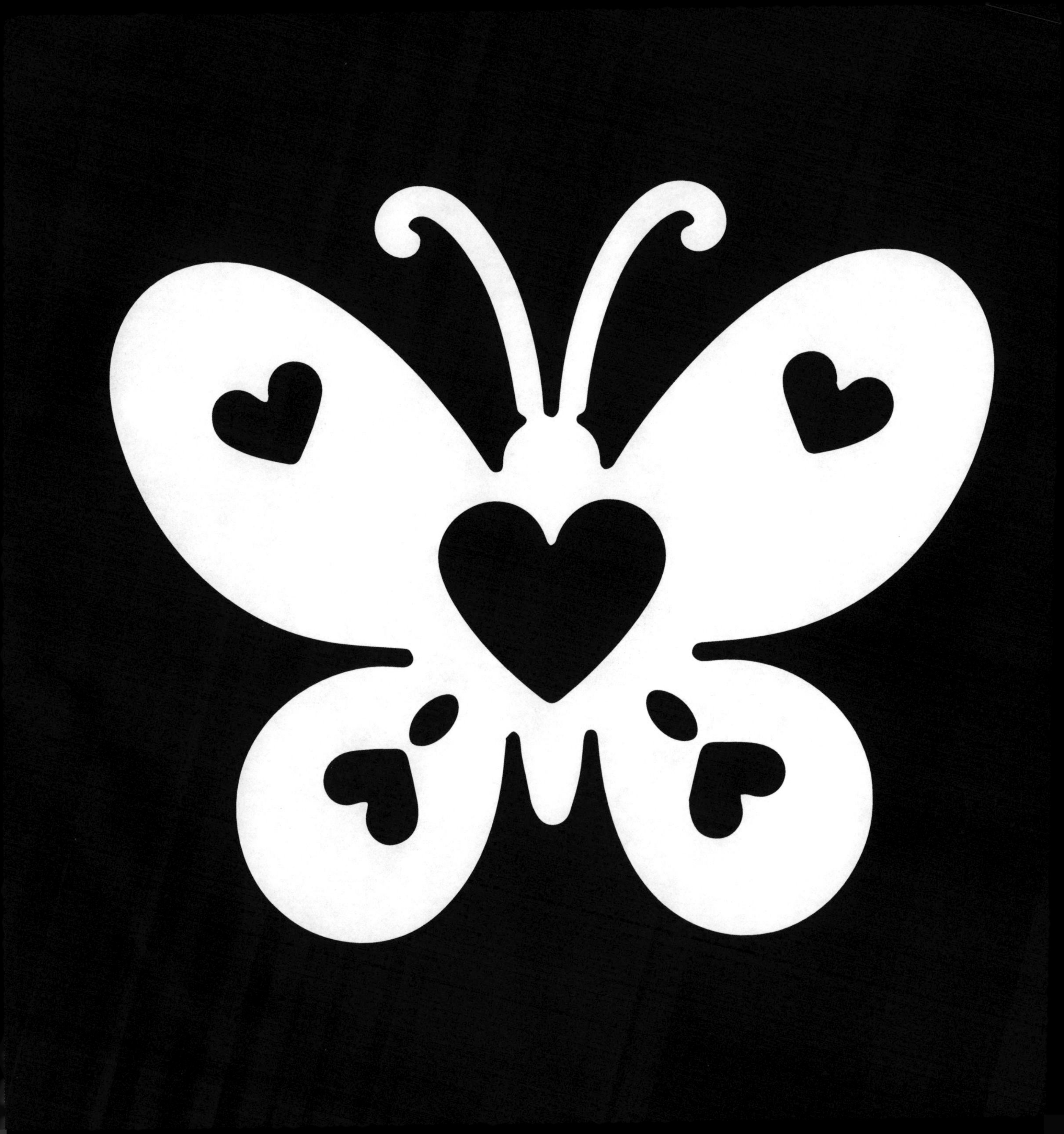

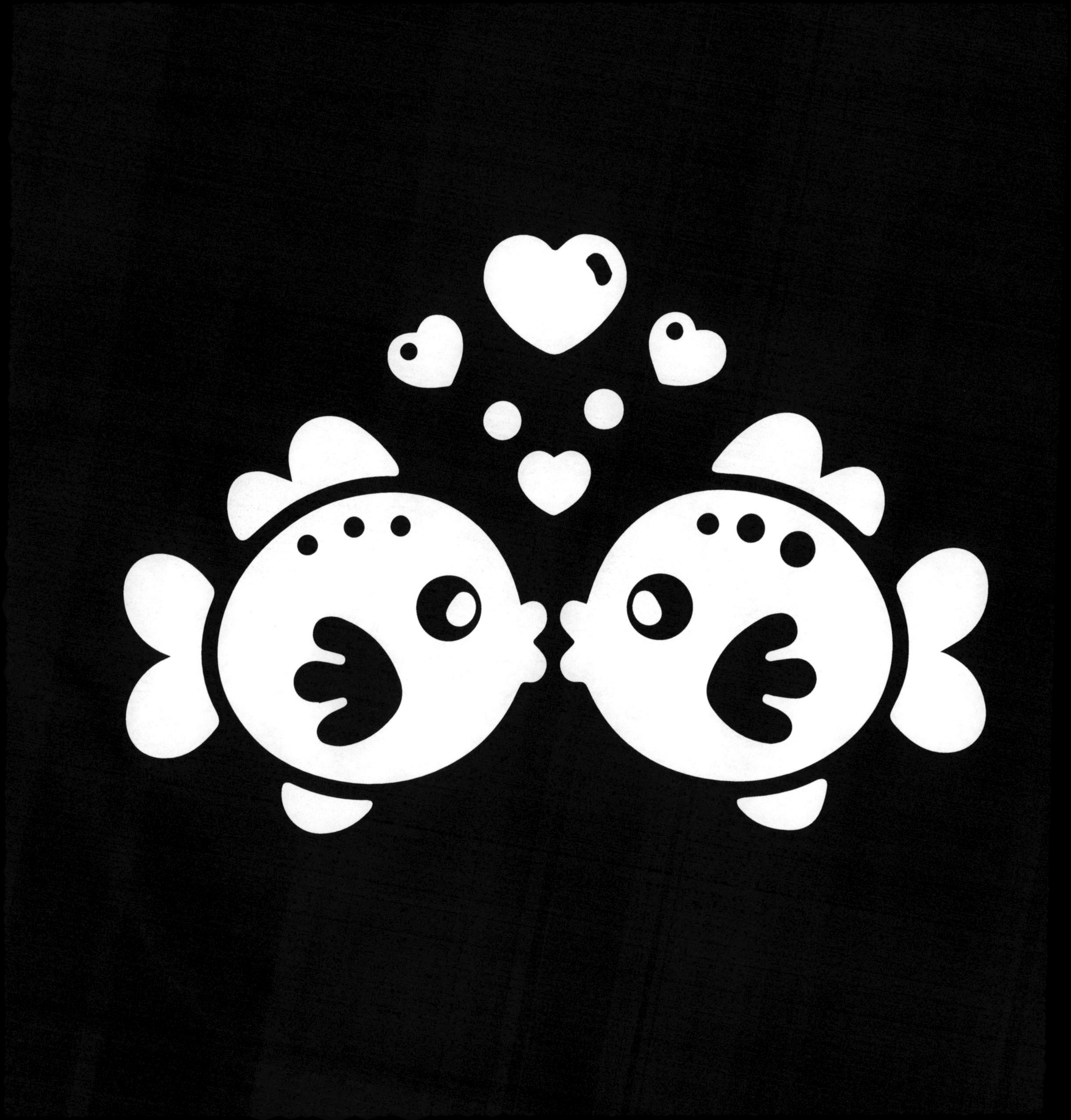

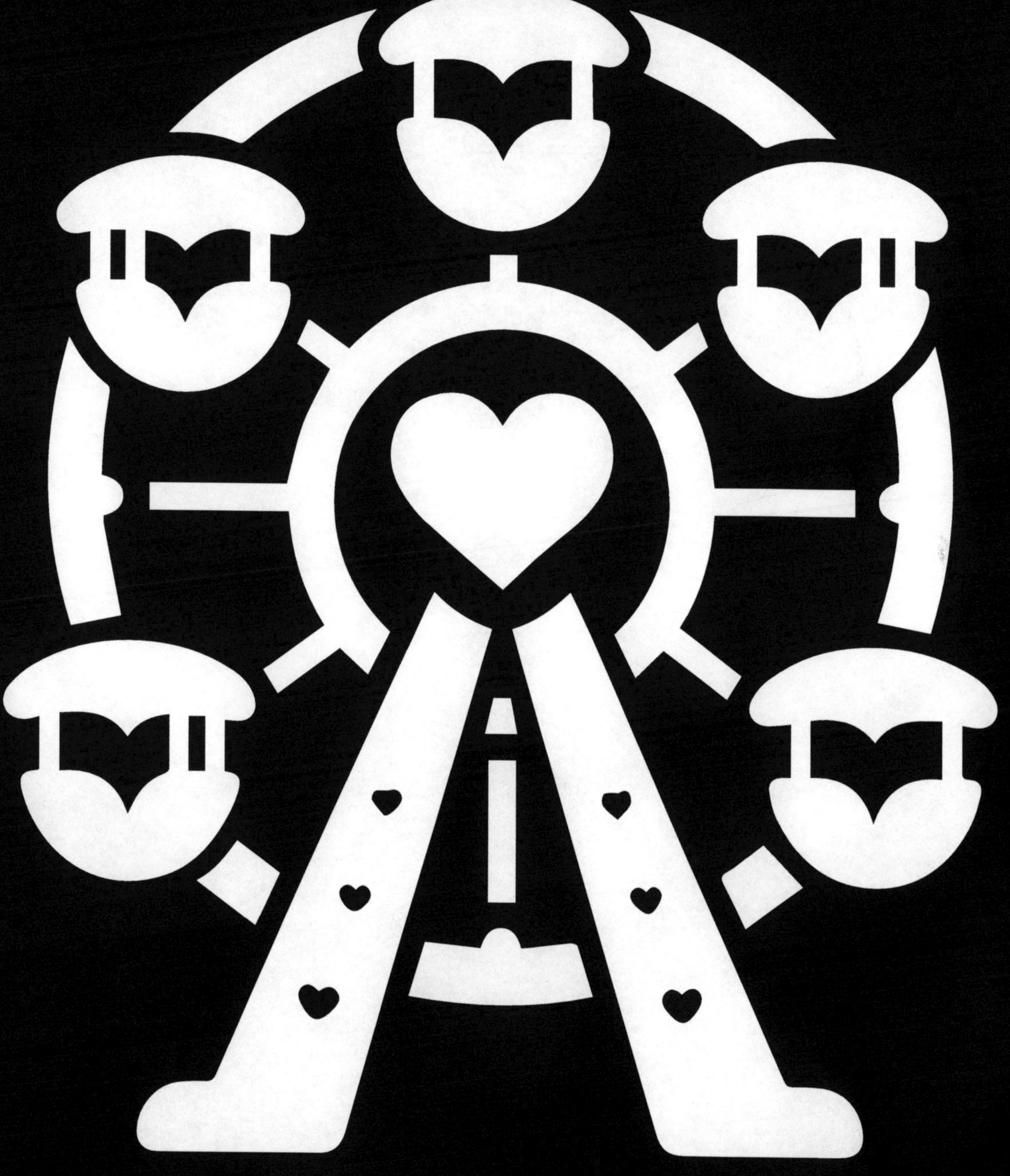

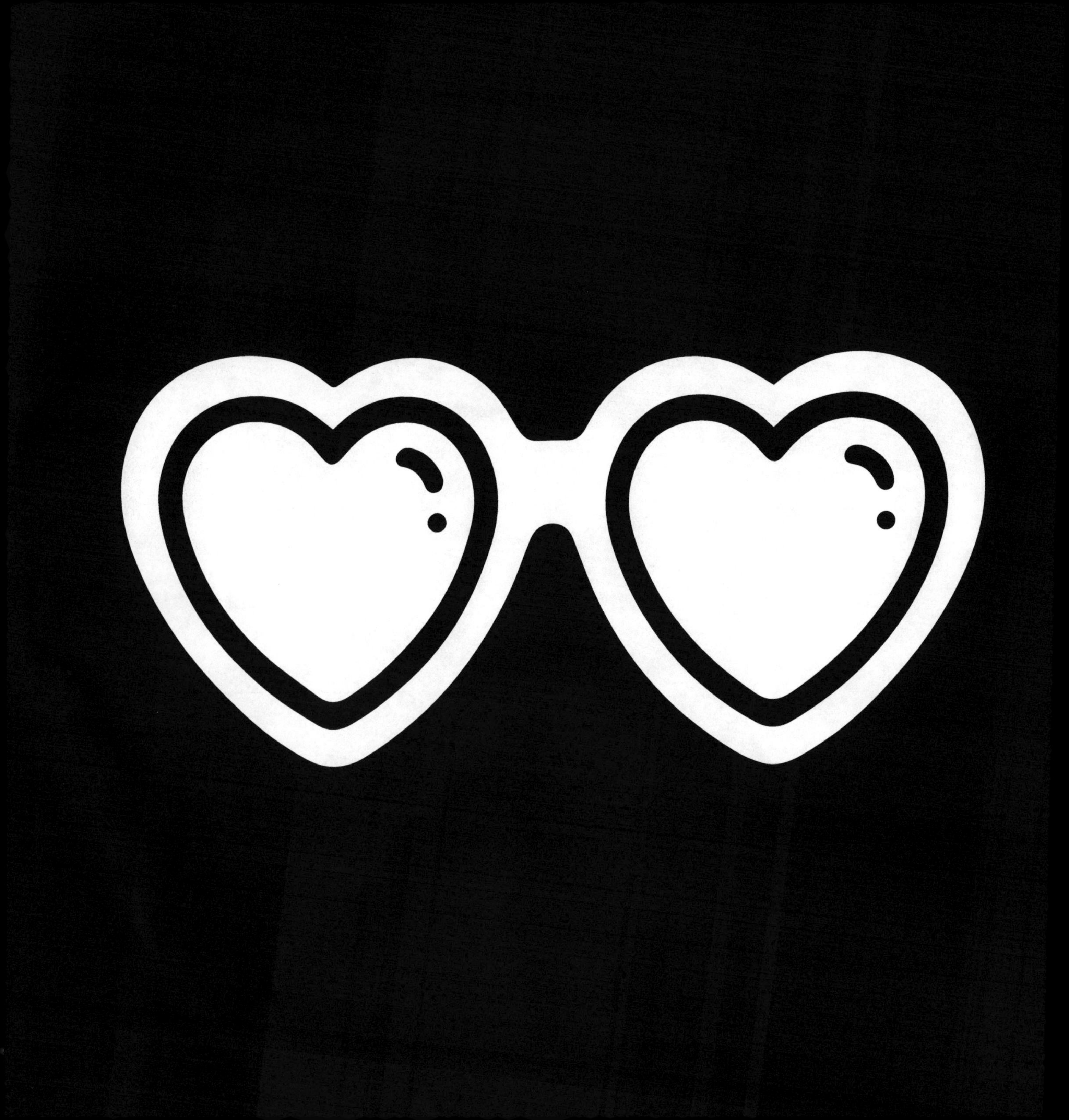

Made in the USA
Monee, IL
06 February 2024

53013570R00022